I0192301

Parenting Special Needs Children

A Christian Guide to Parenting Children with ADHD, Autism, Asperger's, and other Psychological, Behavioral, or Physiological Disorders

By: Patrick Baldwin

Copyright 2017
American Christian Defense Alliance, Inc.
Baltimore, Maryland
ACDAInc.Org

All Rights Reserved. No part of this publication may be reproduced in any form or by any means, including scanning, photocopying, or otherwise without prior written permission of the copyright holder.

Special Request

Thank you for purchasing our book and supporting our Ministry. We actually have two requests – To Pray for Our Ministry and to Read this Book All the Way through. No Ministry can Survive without Prayers and Support so we ask you to keep our Ministry in Your Daily Prayers and Pray as the Lord leads.

We encourage you to Read the Book you purchased all the way through. Many Books NEVER Get Read, and the ones that do only get read the first few pages.

One of our Special Request is that if you are serious about learning the material in this book that you take time to actually read this book in its entirety – all the way through.

We all lead such busy lives nowadays and can get side tracked so easily, please take a moment to consider my words and read to the end of the book and keep us in Your Prayers.

Thank You once again for purchase. We deeply appreciate Your Prayers and Support and know that God will Bless You as You continue to Bless this Ministry.

Dedication

This book is dedicated to the Parents of Special Needs Children and all those that help support you. May you continue to be a light in the darkness guiding the way. Your courage, perseverance, faith and love reflect the best attributes that all parents should strive for – God Bless You and Your Family.

Forward

Having worked for close to 20 years with those in our society that are considered some of the most vulnerable, I wanted to write this book to offer Biblical Guidance for the Christian Parent.

Often times we may become overwhelmed with the thoughts, responsibilities, and day to day grind that having a special needs child can bring to your life. It is critical to see Your Child through the Eyes of God and to Keep Your Focus on Jesus Christ along the Way.

I truly Pray that this book will be a Blessing to You and Your Family and hope that You will share it with other Christian Parents who may be also dealing with the challenges of Parenting a Special Needs Child.

God Bless You

Table of Contents

Chapter 1: You Are Going to be the Parent of a Special Needs Child

When we see the little line on the pregnancy test saying there is a baby growing inside of you, the last thing you probably think about (or one of the last things) is whether or not your baby will have special needs when it comes to their physical, mental, or emotional wellbeing.

You aren't thinking about whether or not you will be able to afford special equipment they might need to live. You aren't thinking about what your insurance will and won't cover and what kind of help you can get to make up the difference. You aren't thinking about whether or not your house will 'work' for a wheelchair, if your boss will allow you to work from home or how you will juggle work and five or six doctor's appointments a month (or possibly in a week).

You aren't thinking about the fact that your baby—the one you've just 'met'—is one of the millions of children in this country that will receive some form of special education when he or she goes to school. And that's providing he or she can go to school.

No, you aren't thinking about those things at all. You are thinking about whether the baby is a boy or girl, when the due date will be, who to share the happy news with first (other than your spouse, of course), and you even start rolling possible names around in your mind. In other words, your thoughts are focused on the joy that comes from bringing a new baby into this world.

Well guess what? Bringing a new baby into this world regardless of whether or not they have special needs *is* a joy. Each and every tiny little life that takes their first breath after working their way into this world is a cause for celebration and joy *because* we are all fearfully and wonderfully made by the LORD God, our Creator.

Nevertheless, learning your child has special needs—whether you find out prior to or immediately after their birth, or a few months or years down the road—is difficult.

Your love for your child instinctively wants them to be 'normal'. You don't want them to have to struggle. You don't want them to have to go through the experience of feeling different from the rest of the kids or to experience the loneliness often felt from being left out of so many things kids like to do. You don't want to see the hurt in their eyes and know their hearts are breaking when they are made fun of or ostracized by their peers.

What's more, you can't help worrying about how their condition or circumstances is going to affect your life and the lives of other family members. And then you start feeling guilty for feeling and thinking that way; making you even more anxious.

Am I right? You know I am. But the GREAT news is that it is perfectly normal and okay to feel and think these things—as long as you are near enough to Jesus to dump it all at His feet so that he can replace all of those things with what you need in order to do the very special job you have been given by God to do.

That's right—being given the responsibility of parenting a child with special needs is NOT a form of discipline or punishment. Instead, God is saying, "I have a special job for you because your heart's capacity to love and nurture is above and beyond what is normal. I created you with the ability to see beyond the obvious into the heart and soul of one of my children, so I need you to raise them up for me."

We see this truth in the Gospel of John, chapter nine, when Jesus heals a man who had been born blind.

Jesus and His disciples were coming into a village when they saw the man, who was most likely begging in front of the marketplace or along the road that led into the village. When the disciples saw that he was blind, they asked Jesus whether it was he or his parents whose sin had caused him to be born blind. (That's the punishment 'thing' I just mentioned.)

Jesus immediately replied that neither the sins of the man nor those of his parents had caused his blindness. And then in the next breath, Jesus added these words: Jesus answered, "Neither this man nor his parents sinned, but that the works of God should be revealed in him..." (John 9:3)

Did you get that? The man's blindness wasn't a curse or punishment. He had been born blind so that he could be an instrument through which Jesus' holiness and power could be displayed. He was literally a partner in Jesus' ministry!

So while parenting a special-needs child maybe wasn't what you anticipated doing as a parent, and while you may feel completely overwhelmed and even terrified at the prospect of doing so, don't let these feelings rob your child of the joy he or she deserves to feel in your touch and see in your eyes that says, "I'm so glad you are mine." And whatever you do, don't let these feelings rob you of the joy you deserve to experience in becoming and being a parent and of the blessing of being God's partner in showing the world just how Holy and Mighty He is.

Bible Verses to Encourage You

And not only that, but we also glory in tribulations, knowing that tribulation produces perseverance; 4 and perseverance, character; and character, hope.
~Romans 5:3-4

And the Lord said unto him, who hath made man's mouth? or who maketh the dumb, or deaf, or the seeing, or the blind? have not I the Lord? ~Exodus 4:11

For thou hast possessed my reins: thou hast covered me in my mother's womb. I will praise thee; for I am fearfully and wonderfully made: marvelous are thy works; and that my soul knoweth right well. ~Psalm 139:13-14

Lo, children are an heritage of the Lord: and the fruit of the womb is his reward.
~Psalm 127:3

Chapter 2: Guarding Your Heart, Soul, Mind, and Strength

You can have all the joy, joy, joy, joy down in your heart, in your head, and bubbling up out of your soul imaginable but that won't erase the fact that parenting a special-needs child is hard work. It is physically exhausting, mentally and emotionally draining, time-consuming, and often times very, very lonely. I think it's safe to say that this is one of those things about which your grandma would say, "The most worthwhile jobs we do are the hardest jobs we do".

Because there is so much required of you, it is important that you take care of yourself. *Good* care of yourself. This is something many parents of special-needs children don't do a very well.

Generally speaking, parents put the needs of their children in front of their own needs—as we should in many instances, but not *all*. And when you take into consideration that the demands on your life because of the increased needs of your child…. I guess you could say that parents of special-needs children have some special needs of their own.

What you are about to read is a list of things you need to be doing for YOURSELF. Don't make excuses and the words "I can't" are not allowed—not even in your head or under your breath. Taking good care of yourself is key to doing your job to the best of your ability and key to knowing you, too, are fearfully and wonderfully made (Psalm 139).

1: Spend time in the Word daily

Ten or fifteen minutes spent reading the Bible each day is food for the soul, body, and mind. Don't just focus on the Psalms or the Gospels—books of the Bible that are usually viewed as the 'feel good' books of the Bible. While you *do* need to make them part of your Bible study, they shouldn't be the only part.

When you spend time in the books of history you become more grounded and sure of the fact that God does have a plan.

The books of Job and Ecclesiastes humble you and remind you that the most important things in life aren't things and that God really does have the whole world (including you and your child) in His hands.

The book of Esther gives us an extra dose of courage and reminds us that our ultimate purpose is to bring Glory to God through all we do and say.

The prophets don't spare words. They tell it like it is when it comes to reminding us that we are all sinners. But they are equally eloquent when it comes to reminding us of God's abundant love and mercy—love and mercy we can draw on every…single…day.

James and most of Paul's letters are the books that keep us on the straight and narrow. They define Christian character, warn us of the consequences for living outside of God's laws and expectations, and reaffirm the promises of heaven in all its glory when we abide in Jesus Christ.

Read God's Word. Apply it to your life. Let it speak to you. Let it change you.

2: Pray

One of the biggest concerns and complaints of parents with special-needs children is that they don't have many people they can talk to who really 'gets' it. Not on a regular basis, that is, because the parents who *do* 'get' it are as busy as they are. But God always hears and He is always available. No, He's not someone you can sit around the table with over a cup of coffee or someone you can chat with while you take a lap or two around the block. But He *is* there, He *does* listen, and He *does* care.

You also need to know (or be reminded of the fact) that your conversations are not one-sided. God responds to you. He responds by:

- Telling the Holy Spirit what to say to you (Jon 16:13)
- Speaking to you through the Scriptures
- Providing answers through your conversations and interactions with others – Something called Confirmation.

In 1 Thessalonians 5:17 we are told to pray without ceasing. If you do that, you'll also be conversing with God nonstop.

3: Eat a healthy diet

God created our bodies to operate at optimum efficiency and capacity when we feed our bodies a steady diet of the food He created for us to eat. Meat, fruits, veggies, dairy products, grains…the things He created to fuel our bodies.

Sure there are exceptions—food allergies and personal tastes, for example. But for the most part you really need to make sure your diet consists primarily of foods free of chemicals, dyes, and processing.

If you are still looking for things like chips, blooming onions, mocha latte caramel coffee with an extra shot of caffeine, diet soda, and seven-layer lasagna on the list of best foods, you can stop. They aren't there. They never will be.

Eating a healthy diet keeps your body working the way it should. Your heart is healthier. Your body doesn't produce a lot of bad fat for you to carry around. You think more clearly. You reduce your risk of getting things like heart disease, diabetes, kidney failure, and bone and joint disorders due to carrying around too much weight. You have more energy. Your immune system does a better job of fighting off colds and the flu.

Question: What's not to like about the benefits of eating a healthy diet?

Answer: Nothing. So do it!

4: Get plenty of exercise

If your child has physical limitations that require you to bathe them, dress them, and help them move from one place to another, you are undoubtedly getting quite a bit of physical activity. But that doesn't mean you don't need to get twenty minutes or so of walking, yoga, aerobics, or whatever else you like to do at least three days a week.

If at all possible, you should also set aside an hour or two each week for more rigorous exercise. A few possible options include: Water aerobics, tennis, volleyball, working out at the gym, swimming laps, or anything else you enjoy that gets your heart pumping.

The physical benefits of exercise go without saying and should be reason enough to make sure you get this time each week. But the physical benefits are just the tip of the proverbial iceberg.

So what are the benefits?

- Exercise increases oxygen to the brain; helping you clear your head and think more rationally and clearly.
- Exercise releases endorphins. Endorphins are hormones that send messages to the brain that tell the brain to think positive thoughts. Endorphins also lessen our perception of pain. They intercept the signals from our nerves and send the message to the brain that it doesn't hurt as bad as 'all that'.
- Exercise keeps your weight in check and your heart healthy.
- Exercise gives you some much-deserved time off from your responsibilities as a parent. Even if it is only for a few minutes a day, it is worth it.

- Exercise boosts your immune system. This is actually one of the top two or three reasons parents of special-needs children take time to exercise. After all, when parents get sick (especially Mom) chaos at home can quickly ensue. So remember... "An ounce of prevention is worth a pound of cure".
- Some forms of exercise provide you with a social outlet. Even if you and a friend take several laps around the block or park, it still counts as time you can enjoy conversations without interruptions.

5: Date nights and marriage protection

Couples with children—no matter how many and no matter what their needs are—all run the risk of letting parenting, work, money-matters, and everything else push their marriage and its wellbeing to the backburner. But when you add the stresses of raising a special-needs child to the mix, the chances of this happening increase significantly.

The financial burdens that come from having a special-needs child are often very heavy to bear. The primary caregiver (usually Mom) doesn't have a lot of time to just sit and talk. She doesn't always have the luxury of prioritizing how her time is spent. That is usually done for her out of sheer necessity.

That's why as parents of a special-needs child you need to make conscious and consistent effort to have couple time free of ANY talk about home, money, the kids, or anything else that pertains to your daily routine. You need to make a conscious effort to make romantic gestures and let your spouse know they are second only to God.

What? But…our child needs me to do…. Who has time for romance? And since my life pretty much revolves around making sure our kids are taken care of, there's not really much else to talk about.

Oh, but there is. There is plenty to talk about:

- Make plans for a weekend getaway…just the two of you
- Talk about an upcoming event at church
- Talk about some things you would like to make time to do for yourself
- Make plans for a family weekend
- Talk about current events

- Recall memories from your dating years and the early years of your marriage
- Talk about the reasons you love one another
- Talk about long-range goals for your marriage and family
- Talk about something funny you saw on television or at the grocery store
- Make a list of ideas of things you can do to keep your marriage fresh and thriving...and then start doing the things on that list

There are several other things you need to make sure you don't neglect to do in order to keep your marriage safe and fresh. These things include:

- Worshipping together.
- Serving together in your church and community.
- Letting your children see and hear you being (appropriately) affectionate with each other.

- Not allowing your children to play you against one another.
- Making sure you kiss each other good morning, hello, goodbye, and goodnight.
- Telling each other "I love you" every single day.
- Not neglecting your appearance—your 'Sunday best' isn't always necessary, but baggy pants, t-shirts, and a messy-hair-don't-care look doesn't say much about the way you feel about yourself. And if you don't care about yourself, it's hard for other people to do so.
- Taking care of your body.
- Showing an interest in your spouse's job (in and away from the home).
- Making their friends feel welcome in your home.
- Respecting their need for 'me' time and giving them that luxury.

- Making sure 'me' time and 'friend' time never add up to more than the time you spend with your spouse and your family.
- Living with the attitude of submission (for wives) and sacrificial love and leadership (for husbands) as directed in the New Testament book of Ephesians.

7: Fellowship

You need fellowship. You need to spend time with your peers; studying God's Word, socializing, enjoying recreational activities and outings, and just hanging out. Just being yourself.

While there is nothing wrong with part of this fellowship coming in the form of support groups or play groups with other parents of special-needs children, this should not be your *only* outlet.

These groups are can be very beneficial—a lifeline for many of you—but you need to be able to fellowship in ways that address *your* needs and interests…not your child's.

Don't think this is being selfish. It's not. By giving yourself this time you are giving your family a better and you—an energized, more confident, refreshed you. So don't feel guilty about taking some time for a Bible study, a weekly game of golf or tennis, meeting up for coffee and fellowship, a book club, or some other group where you can share your passion for your hobby with others who feel the same.

The amount of time you allow yourself isn't a number that is set in stone. There is no magic number that guarantees your needs will be met. For some, an afternoon, evening, or possibly an entire day (or most of it, anyway) a week is doable.

For others, though, an hour or two a week is a priceless and treasured gift that happens only with a great deal of planning, preparation, and help from others.

Speaking of help...

8: Ask for help

You can't do this on your own. Physically...emotionally...mentally...you need help and support.

The help and support you receive can come from a number of different resources. Some of these resources exist solely for the purpose of helping parents of special-needs children and the children themselves. Other sources of help are people who love and care about you and want to be the hands and feet of Jesus in your life. And you need to let them do that.

Bobby and Shannon were the parents of six year-old twins and a three year-old born without hands—his arms stop just below his elbows. Bobby, Shannon, and all three children are completely comfortable with their life. Even the twins are a great help when it comes to feeding, dressing, and playing with their little brother. But they are hesitant to leave their son in anyone's care other than his grandparents when they came to visit or the physical therapist they met with a couple of hours a week. So other than these two hours a week and four or five visits a year from grandparents, Bobby and Shannon took no time for just the two of them.

Friends from church have offered to take all three of the kids on numerous occasions, but Shannon always made an excuse. Thanks, but no thanks, was the message she conveyed. But then one day, a middle-aged woman at church asked Shannon a question that stopped her in her tracks.

She asked, " Why do you insist on keeping people from doing what Jesus wants them to do?"

"Excuse me," Shannon asked back, somewhat offended. "What do you mean?"

"People in this church, including me, want to be part of your family and want you to be part of ours. We want to minister to your family, get to know you and your kids, let you know you have people who love and care about you. We want to live and love the way Jesus told us to, but you won't let us," was the woman's answer.

Shannon didn't know what to say. She'd never thought about it like that before. She was so focused on not wanting to appear to be a charity case or give people a reason to think they needed to feel sorry for them and their son, that she had completely forgotten that Jesus calls us to love and serve one another.

This woman was right! By not accepting their offers for help and fellowship, they were robbing these people of opportunities to be like Jesus. And what's more, they were robbing themselves of the blessings that come with being a part of a family of believers.

From that day on Shannon and Bobby were more than happy to take people up on their offers to babysit so they could have date nights. And they were equally happy to return the favor by doing the same for other young families in the church. Josephine (the woman who talked to Shannon) and her husband became surrogate grandparents to their children, and relationships were built that will undoubtedly last a lifetime.

Today Shannon and Bobby are the parents for four and grandparents to two. They are also in charge of a parent's night out ministry at their church, because they know what it is like to need help AND they know how important it is for others to be able to offer it.

Besides your church family, other possible resources for help include:

- Healthcare agencies
- Playgroups for children with physical disabilities
- Daycare facilities that cater to children with special needs
- Friends and neighbors
- Support groups (for emotional and mental help you need)

9: Me time

In addition to the time you spend with just your spouse and time spent with your friends and peers, you need to have a few minutes of 'me' time every day. Thirty minutes or so each day to do whatever you want to do by yourself. Take a walk. Soak in the bathtub. Read a book. Bake cookies. Shoot some hoops. Watch television without interruption. Surf the web. Catch up on social media. Do your nails. Take a nap. Whatever you enjoy doing…do it.

The purpose of this time of solitude is to allow you to clear your head and not think about anyone or anything but yourself and what you are doing. This is your time to dream, plan, rest, relax, and even be a bit selfish.

Taking this time each day is so important. Knowing you have this time to look forward to each day helps you keep things in the proper perspective. It prevents you from feeling like you've lost your identity as an individual.

You are God's child. You are a spouse. You are a parent. You are an instrument of God's plan. Your body is the temple of the Holy Spirit. You cannot be and do these things if you are not practicing good self-care, so do it. It is your duty to yourself, your family, and to your God.

Bible Verses to Encourage You

It is vain for you to rise up early, to sit up late, to eat the bread of sorrows: for so he giveth his beloved sleep. ~Psalm 127:2

I will both lie down in peace, and sleep; For You alone, O Lord, make me dwell in safety. ~Psalm 4:8

For I have satiated the weary soul, and I have replenished every sorrowful soul. ~Jeremiah 31:25

There remaineth therefore a rest to the people of God. For he that is entered into his rest, he also hath ceased from his own works, as God did from His. ~Hebrews 4:9-10

Chapter 3: True Love is Devoid of All Pride

Every parent's desire is to make their child's life good, happy, pleasant, and as carefree as possible. And why not? Isn't that just part of what loving someone is all about? But when you have a child with special needs, your quest to give these things to your child usually comes with a few (or a lot) more challenges.

Every parent is charged by God with the task of keeping their children safe and healthy, providing them with food, clothing, and shelter, and loving them unconditionally; nurturing and cherishing them for the treasure they are.

Additionally, parents are responsible for raising their children to:

- Learn to be confident and comfortable with who they are
- Know that we are to be God-pleasers…not people-pleasers
- Recognize sin for what it is and rise above it
- To strive to achieve their goals and dreams

But again, children with special needs have to work a little harder to get the job done, and as their parent, *you* have to work a little harder to help them. Your success in doing so depends on your ability to set aside any prideful feelings you have—consciously or subconsciously.

Denial is not uncommon when you first learn that your child has special needs. These feelings are not necessarily evidence of shame or embarrassment.

More often than not they stem from guilt, concern, and apprehension.

- Did I do something…or not do something that caused this?
- Will my child be able to enjoy at least some of the things a child should?
- Can I be the parent my child needs and deserves?

The reason for the feelings isn't necessarily important. What *is* important is that you set them aside for the sake of everyone involved. Don't let pride keep you from dong what is best for your child.

Early intervention

Denial has been the reason for many children's conditions and disabilities to go undiagnosed as soon as they could and should be. If your child isn't diagnosed as having special needs, then the problem isn't really there, right? Wrong!

Early intervention often makes the difference in how severely their disability affects their life (and yours) and the degree to which they can function.

Parents, pretending or burying your head in the sand accomplishes nothing good. So don't deny your child every chance possible to be high-functioning and/or to receive therapy that allows them to be more mobile and independent. Get help at the first sign that a problem exists.

Your pediatrician will be able to connect you with available resources and information for your particular situation. Make use of them.

Living realistically

Once you know what your child's condition is and what their needs are and will be you need to listen intently and carefully to those who can point you in the right direction to get you and your child the help available to you. When meeting with therapists, doctors, and anyone else involved in your child's care, you might not always like what you hear.

Sometimes parents feel the plan of action isn't aggressive enough. Some feel it is too aggressive. And some think the medical community is too pessimistic in their outlook. These are the parents that believe if their child tries hard enough they can overcome their disability.

EXAMPLE: Jared's mom was thoroughly convinced that putting her son in a classroom for special-needs students that he would never reach his full potential. She believed that if he was in a traditional classroom setting he would work harder to be on a level 'playing field' with the rest of the class.

The problem with this line of thinking is that by putting expectations on Jared he simply cannot meet makes him feel bad about himself and causes him to doubt his ability to succeed. It's like giving a five year-old keys to the car and expecting them to be able to drive.

Your child has enough to deal with because of their special needs. Don't add to that by trying to make them someone they are not and by insinuating that you are ashamed of them or that who they are is not reason enough to love them with your whole heart.

Accept the fact that they have limitations. Accept what those limitations are. Put them in a position to excel to the best of their ability. Celebrate their accomplishments. Love them for who they are.

Be your child's advocate and biggest fan

Today's children are only the second or third generation of children to not be hidden away or ignored just because they have special needs. Prior to this, children with special needs were considered to be disposable and less valuable than their 'normal' peers. Children with special needs and disabilities were often placed in institutions where they did little more than exist. Others were kept at home, but were not allowed to go to school and had little or no social interaction. Think: Boo Radley in *To Kill a Mockingbird.*

Thankfully, though, not every parent 'back then' thought or felt that way…

Neal and Bonita knew something was wrong with their second-born son, Gary, before he turned six months old. He wasn't meeting the developmental milestones for babies his age. But in those days and in their small town, it wasn't easy to get a correct diagnosis. When they did, the words they heard were MULTIPLE SCLEROSIS.

Neal and Bonita were encouraged to put Gary in a 'home' where he could live out his days (which they were told would be less than twenty years) peacefully and out of the harsh and unaccepting public eye. But they didn't want to put their son away.

They knew God didn't make a mistake when he made Gary. They knew he was as treasured and loved as anyone else God created. They also knew that every child with special needs was one of God's precious treasures, too. So with nothing but a determination and passion for wanting to help Gary and others like him to reach their full potential, Neal and Bonita recruited teachers and people who practiced a trade to work in what would now be called a sheltered workshop.

Gary is now an eighty year-old man who has never walked on his own, never ran, played catch, or spoken a word that is understandable by an 'untrained' ear. But he *has* appeared before three different presidents of the United States to champion for the rights of people with disabilities.

He even went to Europe to compete in the Special Olympics, won multiple gold and silver medals in the same, accumulated dozens of bowling trophies, and encouraged countless people just by being himself. But these things were possible only because his parents were his biggest fans and they championed for him with relentless energy, passion, and love.

Don't let anyone make your child feel worthless and unlovable. Believe in them and do whatever you can to make sure they are given every possible and feasible opportunity to reach their full potential.

Bible Verses to Encourage You

For I know the thoughts that I think toward you, saith the Lord, thoughts of peace, and not of evil, to give you a future and a hope.
~Jeremiah 29:11

Now unto Him that is able to do exceeding abundantly above all that we ask or think, according to the power that worketh in us...
~Ephesians 3:20

For we are His workmanship, created in Christ Jesus unto good works, which God hath before ordained that we should walk in them. ~Ephesians 2:10

Chapter 4: Overcoming the Educational Obstacles

Back in the day there was an ad campaign targeting high schoolers in an effort to convince them to pursue a college education. The campaign's slogan was, "A mind is a terrible thing to waste". And it's true, a mind *is* a terrible thing to waste—and that means your child, too.

Depending on where you live, your child's school may or may not be equipped to offer your child the educational resources they need and deserve. This is not something you should waste time being angry or bitter about. In most cases the lack of resources is due to a lack of money and/or a lack of qualified teachers in the district—neither of which will be changed by your anger or bitterness. Instead, be pro-active and take matters into your own hands.

Instead of wasting your time and energy, put it to use by either becoming the resources your child needs or by going beyond the walls of the school to get them.

Here are some possible ways you might do that:

Depending on your child's special needs you might consider homeschooling your child. Or better yet, consider forming a homeschool coop with other special need's parents. This has proven to be especially helpful to both parents and students with needs such as dyslexia, mild autism, sensory problems, auditory processing disorder, and a variety of delayed development issues.

Educating your child in this type of environment allows them to:

- Learn in a less congested environment with fewer distractions and risks of over-stimulation and more personalized attention
- Feel safer and more accepted among their peers
- Receive instruction and training at a pace and in a format that will allow them to thrive and excel

As for parents, working together shares the workload, provides a community of support and encouragement, and it allows you to know you are giving your child the learning environment most conducive to their learning style and capabilities.

Hire a tutor. Homeschooling on any level is not always possible. And quite frankly, it is not always the best route to take. Depending on your child's needs and the resources they have available in their school, you may find that by hiring a tutor your child will be able to stay on course with the mainstream student population.

You don't need to go through a professional service to find a good tutor, though. Retired teachers, teachers who have opted to stay home with their own children, but who are willing to tutor a few hours a week, or college students in need of extra money are all great resources. A tutor gives your child the one-on-one they so often need to get them over the hump and to give them the moral support and encouragement to keep trying.

Specialized schools are available in some areas—usually large cities. These are somewhat expensive, however, but *do* offer the best in special-needs education. If you live near one of these schools don't let the price tag scare you. Funding is sometimes available through scholarship programs or organizations to aid and assist children with special needs.

Public schooling is free and available to children with mild to moderately-severe special needs. Many public schools have excellent programs for children with learning disabilities and a staff of loving, caring, and dedicated teachers. Often time's public schools also offer and allow personal aides or assistants for special-needs students.

The job of a personal aide/assistant is to be their student's constant companion throughout the day; assisting them in whatever ways they need assistance. Some of the things they might do include:

- Reading to them if they cannot read but can comprehend
- Signing for the deaf
- Writing for those that cannot write but are fully able to comprehend and can speak the answers
- Feeding and other personal care

No matter what educational obstacles you encounter or what path you choose for your child, remember…a mind is a terrible thing to waste.

Bible Verses to Encourage You

How much better is it to get wisdom than gold! and to get understanding rather to be chosen than silver! ~Proverbs 16:16

Take firm hold of instruction, do not let go; Keep her, for she is your life.
~Proverbs 4:13

Give instruction to a wise man, and he will be yet wiser: teach a just man, and he will increase in learning. ~Proverbs 9:9

Chapter 5: We Are Family

When asked what challenges a special-needs child brings to the dynamics of a family, the answers are all over the map.

- "I don't think of my child's needs as something that challenges our family," one parent said. "Being a family means seeing one another as equally valuable and loving one another for who we are. So if who we are, is someone who needs help eating or who cannot play ball, then so be it."

- "I find myself working harder than I really need to sometimes to make things equal for my kids. Sometimes I feel guilty about spending more time with my daughter because of her needs, but then God reminds me that not having to do those things for my boys is a good thing."

- "It is challenging. My now-seven year-old was three when an accident left her with some physical disabilities and mild learning disabilities. I was expecting our second child at the time, so adjusting to all the changes in our routine and life in general really did keep me from enjoying my new baby. I am constantly second-guessing myself in regards to how good a mom I am to each of them."

- "I leave for work every morning knowing my wife is on a non-stop schedule. I feel guilty for being gone so much, but our son's medical expenses are over the top. We'll never be able to see the light at the end of the tunnel. We would like to have another child, but don't know how in the world we could handle two. We want to know what it's like to parent a child that doesn't need round the clock care (or close to it). We want to know what it's like to go to our kid's ball game or dance recital. Is that so bad or wrong?"

- We have two boys in school and our four year-old son is low-functioning autistic. The six and nine year old boys are great with him at home, but I've noticed lately they get embarrassed when Judson acts out in public and they say things like, "Can't you just take us and Mom and Judson stay home?" Or "Judson can't do that, so why does he have to come?" I know some of that is natural, but right now I'm really struggling with how to teach my boys to love their brother for who he is and to love him like they love each other."

-

I could say all sorts of things on how I feel or what I think on how to handle the possible challenges a special-needs child can bring to your family. But what I think and how I feel aren't important.

What is important is what God has to say on the subject of family unity…regardless of the physical, mental, or emotional issues that might be present. So take a few minutes to let God's Word soak into your heart and mind. Share these verses with your spouse, your children, and even your extended family members in an effort to remind them that we are ALL created in the image of God and are ALL equally loved and valued by him.

Bible Verses to Encourage You

Love suffers long and is kind; love does not envy; love does not parade itself, is not puffed up; does not behave rudely, does not seek its own, is not provoked, thinks no evil; does not rejoice in iniquity, but rejoices in the truth; bears all things, believes all things, hopes all things, endures all things
~1 Corinthians 13:4-7 (NKJV)

We love him, because he first loved us.
~1 John 4:19

Better is a dry morsel with quietness, Than a house full of feasting with strife.
~Proverbs 17:1

For as we have many members in one body, but all the members do not have the same function, so we, being many, are one body in Christ, and individually members of one another. ~Romans 12:4-5

For the body is not one member, but many. If the foot shall say, because I am not the hand, I am not of the body; is it therefore not of the body? And if the ear shall say, because I am not the eye, I am not of the body; is it therefore not of the body? If the whole body were an eye, where were the hearing? If the whole were hearing, where were the smelling? But now hath God set the members every one of them in the body, as it hath pleased him. ~1 Corinthians 12:15-18

Chapter 6: Let Your "Light" Shine

Remember reading about Neal and Bonita and how they refused to stifle their son, Gary's potential in time when that was the norm for kids like Gary? Thankfully things are much different today.

Today parks have playgrounds for children with even the most severe disabilities.

Today public buildings have rams and entryways that are accessible to people in a wheelchair.

Today public restrooms are equipped with facilities with enough room to maneuver around in and with sinks, toilets, etc. placed at the right height.

Today even campground shower houses have wheelchair-accessible showers.

Today parking lots provide spaces for vehicles with special-needs drivers or passengers.

Today special-needs children can grow up to be special-needs adults who contribute to society in a positive manner by working, volunteering, and just living life to the fullest.

All of these things are definitely improvements over what used to be, but that doesn't mean life for families of special-needs children is not without its share of obstacles in their communities and their social lives.

When it comes to meeting and overcoming the challenges of special-needs children and their families in the community and on the social 'scene', you need to respond the same way you should when it comes to your child's education. You need to be a pro-active advocate instead of an angry, bitter parent.

And the best way to do this is to help the world see what an amazing and precious person your child is. Proverbs 31:8 (NKJV) says: *Open your mouth for the speechless, In the cause of all who are appointed to die.* So do it! Open your mouth, use your hands to open doors, your feet to walk through them, and your mind to think of ways to help your child be a part of the world around them.

Don't hide their light under a basket. Let them shine for all those around them to see...and be blessed.

- Attend church and let your child be involved in the youth program to the extent they are capable of. Be willing to act as a chaperone for youth events so that your child can participate.

- Volunteer with your child. Taking their specific needs into consideration, consider participating in walk-a-thons (or wheel-a-thons, if necessary). Fill shoe boxes with gifts for other children. Ring the Salvation Army bells. Hand out personal care bags to the homeless. Visit a nursing home together.
- Join a play group.
- Visit the park on a regular basis.
- Enroll your child in swimming lessons, bowling lessons, or some other type of activity they are capable of participating in. *Many of these activities/lessons offer special lessons for children with various handicaps.
- Join 4-H, scouts, or another similar type of organization.
- Go to the weekly story hour at your library.

- Participate in free movie nights, craft-making events, kid-friendly lectures and demonstrations, etc. offered in your community.
- Go for ice cream or an occasional dinner at a favorite family pizza place or restaurant.
- Get them involved with Special Olympics.

The "Bible Verses to Encourage You" segments in previous chapters have already listed Exodus 4:11 and Psalm 139:13-14, but I want us to look at them again because they are important reminders to everyone that God creates each of us in his image and with a distinct set of purposes in mind. Special-needs children are not mistakes. God doesn't make mistakes. Special-needs children are special-*purposes* children and as their parents you need to help them accomplish those purposes in this world.

Bible Verses to Encourage You

And the Lord said unto him, who hath made man's mouth? or who maketh the dumb, or deaf, or the seeing, or the blind? have not I the Lord? ~Exodus 4:11

For thou hast possessed my reins: thou hast covered me in my mother's womb. I will praise thee; for I am fearfully and wonderfully made: marvelous are thy works; and that my soul knoweth right well. ~Psalm 139:13-14

But indeed, O man, who are you to reply against God? Will the thing formed say to Him who formed it, "Why have you made me like this?" ~Romans 9:20

Chapter 7: Dealing With Special Social and Communication Needs

Children with social and communication special needs are those with autism, Asperger, and ADHD (as well as a few others). But then you already know that, don't you? You know that your child has difficulties interacting socially and communicating their thoughts and needs.

The severity of these conditions varies widely from person to person. In some children it is a matter of controlling their intake of certain foods and providing them with a structured environment so that they don't feel (and act) like a loose cannon. But for others, the problem is much more intense. Some children cannot speak or communicate on any level.

Some children cannot handle even slight changes in their routine without becoming unsettled and sometime nearly impossible to manage or console. But again, you already know these things.

What you don't know...or need to be reminded of is that neither you nor your child is alone in the struggles you are facing to deal with life as you know it. God is ever-present.

His presence is visible in the words of the Bible:

He healeth the broken in heart, and bindeth up their wounds. ~Psalm 147:3

*It is of the Lord's mercies that we are not
consumed, because His compassions fail
not. They are new every morning: great is
thy faithfulness. The Lord is my portion,
saith my soul; therefore will I hope in Him.
The Lord is good unto them that wait for
Him, to the soul that seeketh him.*
~Lamentations 3:22-25

*But God commendeth His love toward us, in
that, while we were yet sinners, Christ died
for us. ~Romans 5:8*

Another means by which God proves His
presence is in providing resources and
counsel for you and your child.

Because God has worked through others, we know that parents of children with autism and ADHD can help their child when they:

- Provide a consistent routine and schedule for their child
- Make home a safe, fun, and hazard-free place to be
- Make time for fun; doing things THEY enjoy doing
- Reward positive behavior
- Discover their child's triggers for tantrums and melt-downs and then take necessary actions and precautions
- Know the child's sensitivities (smell, sound, etc.) and try to avoid them or forewarn them
- Concentrate on the child's strengths; allowing them to achieve and excel
- Teach older children to use public transportation, tech gadgets, and other helps in order to be more independent
- Teach them to respect themselves
- Teach them to love, honor, and obey the LORD

Parents of children with Asperger's can help their children by:

- Help your child practice appropriate reactions to common social situations at home so they can learn without feeling judged or on display.
- Teach your children the meaning of common phrases that aren't meant to be taken literally, since many children with Asperger's are quite literal. Example: Telling a child with Asperger's that he is silly will often get this type of response: "I'm not silly, I'm Max."
- Give your child a safety phrase—something to say that will alert you that they are feeling anxious and scared and unsure of how to respond or react.
- Prevent situations when possible rather than try to cure them after the fact.

- Plan ahead and keep your child informed of what they can expect. Surprises and the unexpected are NOT enjoyable to them.
- Don't argue with your child. Negotiate or end the conversation until both of you are better able to communicate rationally.
- Let them 'run with' the things that interest them and don't try to squelch their methods of imaginary play.

Whatever level of function your child has, remember this: They are precious in God's sight and are significant to His plan.

Chapter 8: Dealing With Special Neurological Needs

In an effort to encourage you to stay the course and keep things in their proper perspective, I want to offer you a list of tips and suggestions for dealing with the special needs of your child in a way that will benefit them and the rest of your family.

Remember: Every child deserves to know, beyond a doubt, that the only reason you *need* to love them is because they are yours—that that's enough to merit your unconditional love.

Keeping that in mind, here are some things you can do to help your child with sensory processing disorder:

- Slow down. A lot of times children will be able to accept and enjoy new experiences if they are allowed to approach them at a slower pace.
- Give them space. Again, they need time to adjust to their surroundings and assess them in their own way.
- Keep things as visual as possible, as kids with sensory disorders are usually calmed by what they can see.
- Keep a bag full of items to distract your kids from sensory overload handy at ALL times.
- Be sensitive to their thoughts, feelings, and needs. Don't force things on them that aren't necessary.
- Introduce new sights, sounds, textures, and smells in a positive manner. Teach them to try something new, but let their response be the indicator of how far to take it.

- A therapy or specialized play group can be beneficial. Sometimes positive peer pressure works for the good of your child.

Children with auditory processing disorder:

- Should receive instructions in short, simple sentences. One step at a time.
- Should always be spoken to when facing them and when you are sure you have their attention.
- Keep things as visual as possible. Use chore charts, to-do lists, etc.
- Ask questions like: "Do you understand?" "Do you know what you are supposed to do?" "What did I just say to you?" Ask these questions in a loving, affirmative tone—not one that is condescending and degrading.
- Provide your child with simple puzzles, I-spy books, and toys that produce visible results.

Children with Tourette's and Epilepsy:

- Make sure your child takes their medication on schedule.
- Have regular medical checkups and evaluations.
- Make sure everyone in the family, teachers, and caregivers know what to do in the event of a seizure.
- Educate those who live and work with your child on the facts about Tourette's, Epilepsy, or other neurological disorder.
- Remember that the vast majority of children with Tourette's and Epilepsy have no mental or emotional disabilities. They are what society considers high-functioning children.
- Children with Epilepsy should always wear helmets when riding a bike or skating.

- Never allow an epileptic child to swim alone or be left alone in the tub. Older children should not be allowed to take a bath…showers only.
- Make sure your child has a medical alert bracelet or necklace on in the event they require emergency care and you are not with them. This will allow those around them to get the help your child needs.

REMEMBER: Awareness and knowledge are your child's two best allies when it comes to living with and thriving in spite of their special needs.

Bible Verses to Encourage You

You also, as living stones, are being built up a spiritual house, a holy priesthood, to offer up spiritual sacrifices acceptable to God through Jesus Christ. 1 Peter 2:5 (NKJV)

Be anxious for nothing, but in everything by prayer and supplication, with thanksgiving, let your requests be made known to God; and the peace of God, which surpasses all understanding, will guard your hearts and minds through Christ Jesus. ~Philippians 4:6-7

*Take heed that ye despise not one of these little ones; for I say unto you, that in heaven **their** angels do always behold the face of my Father which is in heaven. ~Matthew 18:10*

Chapter 9: Dealing with Genetic and Physical Special Needs

Among the most common physical and genetic problems facing parents of children with special needs include: cystic fibrosis, multiple sclerosis, cerebral palsy, downs syndrome, congenital birth defects of the vital organs or limbs, dyslexia, and muscular dystrophy.

There are of course, less common and even rare forms of these types of diseases and disorders including, dwarfism and SMA (spinal muscular atrophy)—to name just a few. And then there are those families dealing with special needs resulting from accidental injuries and problems resulting from the birth mother's abuse of drugs and alcohol.

No matter what the cause of the defect, disease, or injury, the fact remains that a child needs and deserves to enjoy the highest quality of life possible. Therefore, it is the wise and caring parent who makes the most of every opportunity and resource to help make that happen. You can be that parent when you:

- No matter what your child's special needs are, make sure everyone who lives with and spends time with your child on a regular basis knows what your child's condition is, what their needs are, has a working knowledge of how to meet those needs, and knows what to do in an emergency as well as how to do it.
- Make sure your child receives regular checkups and evaluations by their doctor and specialists.
- Make sure your child gets adequate rest, exercise (to the best of their ability), and social and intellectual stimulation and interaction.

- Make sure your child is eating a healthy and nutritious diet. Make this a family thing. For example: If your child is diabetic, don't make them feel deprived and different by keeping candy in the house for everyone else. Make it a special treat for everyone—even your diabetic on occasion.

- Be your child's advocate by taking whatever steps are necessary to ensure they receive the education they deserve and the assistance they need to reach their full potential.

- Do your homework. Stay up on the news concerning available resources for your child.

- Realize there are some things your child simply cannot do. When this happens you need to remember two things: 1) don't make your other children miss out on things. Let them enjoy the life they have been given. And 2) don't make a big deal out of it. Instead, focus on the things they *can* do and let them give those things 100%.

Children with Downs's Syndrome

- Embrace and enjoy their loving, affectionate nature.
- Encourage them to participate in social activities.
- Make sure they are receiving the best possible balance of mainstream classroom learning and classes targeted to meet their special needs. Downs kids are not dumb. They just need help learning how to express and use what they know.

- Parents of children with downs need to make exercise and healthy eating a priority to combat their tendency to be overweight and have heart problems.

Children with mobility needs

- Take your child for regular medical checkups and evaluations. Most mobility diseases and defects are progressive in nature; meaning they only get worse over time. You and your child need to know what is going on inside their body in order to meet their changing needs.
- Establish a regular routine for physical therapy. Movement of the right kind is essential for maintaining a quality of life for your child.
- Make sure your home is fully accessible to them. No child should feel unwelcome or in the way in their own home.

- Make sure your home is a safe place for your child. Loose rugs, exposed cords, and furniture that is unsteady can be hazardous.
- Equip your home in such a way that your child can grow into an independent young person. Make sure they can access the microwave and stovetop. Make sure the refrigerator opens in the direction necessary for them to be able to reach things easily. Make sure light switches are reachable. Lower the rods and shelves in their closet. Install a shower or tub to accommodate their needs with minimal or no assistance.

- Provide forms of exercise and entertainment they can enjoy at home: a swing set to accommodate their needs, a hot tub (ONLY with adult supervision), fuse ball, games with little or no physical movement required (trivia, etc.), audio books, and special instruments that will allow them to work the computer, and telephone.
- Take family outings that are wheelchair-friendly. Most state and national parks and sites are, as well as city parks, theaters, and amusement parks.

Children with genetic and other physical limitations

Genetic abnormalities can show themselves physically, mentally, or emotionally. The degree to which they show themselves also varies widely; ranging from things like dyslexia to an inability to speak or breathe without the assistance of a machine.

Because there are so many different forms or levels of special needs your child might have because of these things, it is important that you educate yourself as much as possible in regards to:

- The particulars of your child's needs and condition
- The resources available to you and your child
- What you can and cannot expect in the way of progression or digression
- What you should and shouldn't expect of your child
- How to properly care for your child
- How to help your child reach their full potential

When it's all is said and done, the most important thing you can remember as the parent of a special-needs child is that Jesus loves the little children - ALL the little children of the world – And that means Your Child too.

Bible Verses to Encourage You

Lo, children are a heritage of the Lord: and the fruit of the womb is His reward.
~Psalm 127:3

Behold the fowls of the air: for they sow not, neither do they reap, nor gather into barns; yet your heavenly Father feedeth them. Are ye not much better than they?
~Matthew 6:26

for I was hungry and you gave Me food; I was thirsty and you gave Me drink; I was a stranger and you took Me in; I was naked and you clothed Me; I was sick and you visited Me; I was in prison and you came to Me.

*"Then the righteous will answer Him, saying, 'Lord, when did we see You hungry and feed You, or thirsty and give You drink? When did we see You a stranger and take You in, or naked and clothe You? Or when did we see You sick, or in prison, and come to You?' And the King will answer and say to them, '***Assuredly, I say to you, inasmuch as you did it to one of the least of these My brethren, you did it to Me.***'.*
~*Matthew 25:35-40*

Chapter 10: Your Not-So-Secret Secret Thoughts

As the parent of a special-needs child you have thoughts and feelings parents of other kids don't have. You think:

- Why my child? Why don't they get to run and play? Why can't they enjoy something as simple as licking an ice cream cone or sloshing through a mud puddle in their bare feet? Why do they have to be the one kids make fun of and shy away from?

- Why doesn't God answer my prayers to heal my child? He healed all those other people in the Bible?

- If I hear the term 'short bus', 'retard', or 'freak' one more time I'm going to explode all over whoever says it.

- I just wish I could have one day that was the kind of normal most people have.

- I know they say it's not my fault, but…but…is it…maybe?

And yes, some of you have even thought:

- If we wouldn't have had this to deal with, our marriage would have survived.
- It's not fair to my other children for me to have to devote so much of myself to their sibling.
- My husband or wife and I are never going to know what it's like to be just the two of us.
- What's going to happen to him/her when we can no longer take care of him/her? Who will take over?
- I'm so tired I don't know if I can do this again tomorrow.

You are only human, so it is natural for you to become weary, worried, and worn down. But the great news is—the news you *have to hold tight to*—is that you don't have to remain weary, worried, and worn down. God the Father, Jesus the Son, and the Holy Spirit are here to help. They are here to take these things from you and replace them with rest, peace, and hope.

As we close out our 'time' together, I want to leave you with some final words of encouragement from the scripture. My prayer is that these words will inspire you to be thankful for and mindful of the fact that you have been chosen by God to care for and rise up one of his extra-special children.

God bless you abundantly!

Bible Verses to Encourage You

Casting down arguments and every high thing that exalts itself against the knowledge of God, bringing every thought into captivity to the obedience of Christ;
~2 Corinthians 10:5

Finally, brethren, whatever things are true, whatever things are noble, whatever things are just, whatever things are pure, whatever things are lovely, whatever things are of good report, if there is any virtue and if there is anything praiseworthy—meditate on these things. ~Philippians 4:8

I beseech you therefore, brethren, by the mercies of God, that you present your bodies a living sacrifice, holy, acceptable to God, which is your reasonable service. And do not be conformed to this world, but be transformed by the renewing of your mind, that you may prove what is that good and acceptable and perfect will of God.
~Romans 12:1-2

Special Gift

God has a Gift for You!   The Plan of
Salvation:

There is no formal prayer of salvation as
many churches would have you believe,
God's Word is very clear - there is only one
way to get to the Father in heaven and that is
through Jesus Christ (John 14:6). Jesus says
that you must be born again to enter into
heaven (John 3:3-5).

Salvation is simply the first step in building
an open and honest relationship with God.
We all have sinned and fallen short, but
there is Hope in Jesus Christ - Just cry out to
God in sincerity and honesty asking for
forgiveness and for Him to Save you,
Sanctify you, and fill you with His Holy
Spirit - Ask for His will to be done in your
life on earth as it is in Heaven and That's it,
now just keep it real with God.

A Warning:

The Christian walk is not an easy life on the surface. The Word of God says that we will be hated in all the world for Christ namesake (Matt. 24:9). The Bible says that in the last days are enemy prevail against us physically until Christ returns to save us (Dan 7:21, 22). Furthermore, we must endure hardship as a good soldier of Jesus Christ (2 Tim 2:3) and yet we are never alone in this, God promises us that He will never leave us nor forsake us if we believe in him (Matt.28:20).

In everything we go through we have the peace and joy of God which surpasses all understanding (Philp. 4:6-8) The Bible declares, "For I consider the sufferings of this present time are not worthy to be compared with the glory which shall be revealed in us". (Rom 8:18). However, in all these things we are more than conquerors through Jesus Christ (Rom. 8:37)

Stay In Contact

Stay in Contact with the American Christian Defense Alliance, Inc. through Our Website At: .ACDAInc.Org

Join Our Mailing List

We also Greatly Appreciate You Signing Up For Our Mailing List and Providing a Good Rating and review for this Book. Your reviews help other people like yourself find this book on Amazon and benefit from its contents.

If You or Your Family have been Blessed by this book please let us know by dropping us a line through our website at ACDAInc.Org

Find All Our Books

Some of Our Books:

Parenting: How To Be A Great Parent And Raise Awesome Kids

Prayer: Your No. 1 Prayer Book To Learn To Be A Strong Christian Prayer Warrior That Prays With Powerful Prayers In The War Room To Overcome And Defeat The Enemy

Salvation for Your Unsaved Mom: 10 Things to Tell Your Mom Before She Dies

Wisdom from Your Elders: Learning From Your Parents, Grandparents, and the Older People in Your Church

Kids and Prayer: Pray with Your Kids and Teach Them How to Pray

Embracing Pregnancy, Your Child, and Parenting: A Christian Parenting Guide to Offer Encouragement During the Wonders, Joy, and Hope of Your First Child

Race Relations in America: A Christian Guide to Unite Christians in the Faith

Martial Arts Ministry: How To Start A Martial Arts Ministry

Biblical Bug Out: Don't Bug In - Follow The Calling

Christian Prepping 101: How To Start Prepping

How to Finance Your Full-Time RV Dream

Make Money: A Beginners Guide to Start an Online Business, Work from Home, Make Money, and Develop Financial Freedom

Additional Platforms

Thank you for reading this book. Your support and the support of others continue to enable our Ministry to grow. We hope and pray that this book has blessed you. If you enjoyed this book consider purchasing it on additional platforms or giving it as a gift to someone who could benefit from it.

We have this book available as an E-Book, Paperback, and Audio Book. We have no way to know which platform you purchased our book on but want to make you aware of another way you can help support our Ministry if you haven't yet listen to the audio book version of this book.

If you Enjoy Listening to Audio Books in General Consider Signing Up For Audible.com.

If You've Been On the Fence About Signing Up for Audible.com or Would Just like to Support Our Ministry By Purchasing Our Audio Book First – We Would Greatly Appreciate It.

Did You Know that You Can Support Our Ministry By Listening to Our Audio Books on Audible.com?

Here's How:

- Sign Up as a New Aubdible.com Member

- Purchase Our Audio Book First and

- Stay an Audible.com Member for at least 61 Days

If You Follow these Simple Steps Our Ministry will Earn $25.00 - $50.00 Every Time This Process in Completed. The Amount we earn is based on if we have narrated the book ourselves or outsourced it to another narrator.

We Greatly Appreciate Your Support as
Well as You Sharing this information,
including links to our books on Audible.com
with Others on Your Social Media Platforms

Thank You Once Again for Your Support;
We Know God Will Bless You as You Have
Blessed This Ministry

www.ingramcontent.com/pod-product-compliance
Lightning Source LLC
Chambersburg PA
CBHW032020090426
42741CB00006B/682